PICTURE LIBRARY

POLAR ANIMALS

PICTURE LIBRARY

POLAR ANIMALS

Norman Barrett

Franklin Watts

London   New York   Sydney   Toronto

© 1988 Franklin Watts Ltd

First published in Great Britain
    1988 by
Franklin Watts Ltd
12a Golden Square
London W1R 4BA

First published in the USA by
Franklin Watts Inc
387 Park Avenue South
New York
NY 10016

First published in Australia by
Franklin Watts
14 Mars Road
Lane Cove
NSW 2066

UK ISBN: 0 86313 643 5
US ISBN: 0-531-10531-8
Library of Congress Catalog Card
Number 87-50851

Printed in Italy

Designed by
Barrett & Willard

Photographs by
Survival Anglia
Pat Morris
N.S. Barrett Collection

Illustrations by
Rhoda & Robert Burns

Technical Consultant
Michael Chinery

Contents

Introduction

Polar animals are animals that live in the polar regions of the earth. These are the areas of ice and snow and the cold waters around the North and South poles.

The polar bear is perhaps the best known of the animals that live in the Arctic around the North Pole. But there are many others, including musk oxen and caribou, smaller animals such as hares and foxes, and birds such as ptarmigan and owls.

△ A polar bear cub follows its mother across the icy snows of the Arctic region. Mother bears protect their young and teach them to hunt for food.

The south polar region is Antarctica. Several kinds of penguins live in the southern seas. They come ashore to nest on the continent of Antarctica and on the islands and ice shelves of the region. Many other birds also live in Antarctica in the summer.

Some kinds of whales and seals are found in both polar regions, and a bird called the Arctic tern migrates from the Arctic to the Antarctic to enjoy two summers.

△ A huge elephant seal sleeps on an island beach in Antarctica, while a group of king penguins waddles past.

7

Looking at polar animals

Many animals move to the tundra when
it thaws during
the summer.

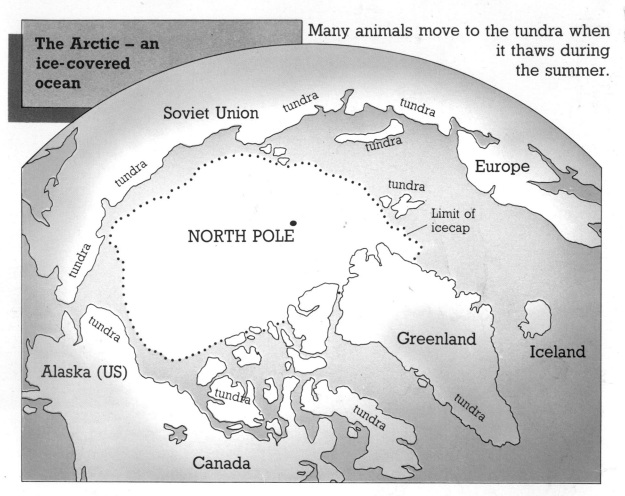

Soviet Union

tundra

tundra

tundra

Europe

tundra

tundra

Limit of
icecap

NORTH POLE

Greenland

Iceland

Alaska (US)

tundra

tundra

tundra

tundra

Canada

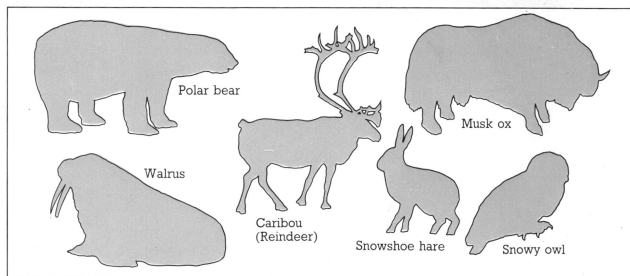

Polar bear

Musk ox

Walrus

Caribou
(Reindeer)

Snowshoe hare

Snowy owl

The Antarctic – a frozen continent

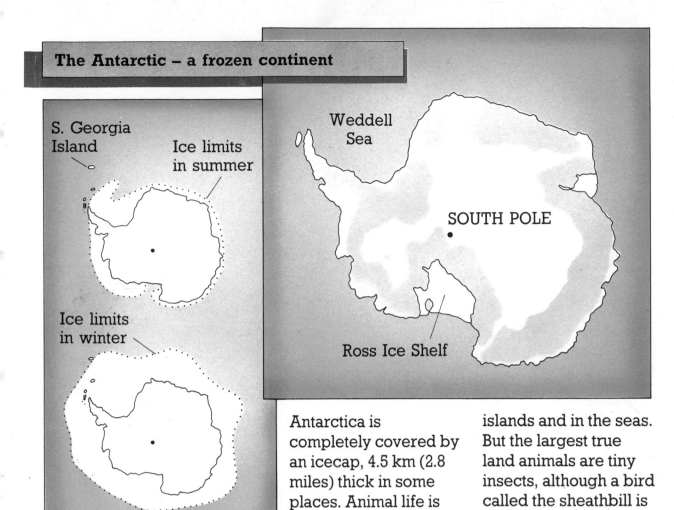

S. Georgia Island

Ice limits in summer

Ice limits in winter

Weddell Sea

SOUTH POLE

Ross Ice Shelf

Antarctica is completely covered by an icecap, 4.5 km (2.8 miles) thick in some places. Animal life is found on the coasts and islands and in the seas. But the largest true land animals are tiny insects, although a bird called the sheathbill is a native of the region.

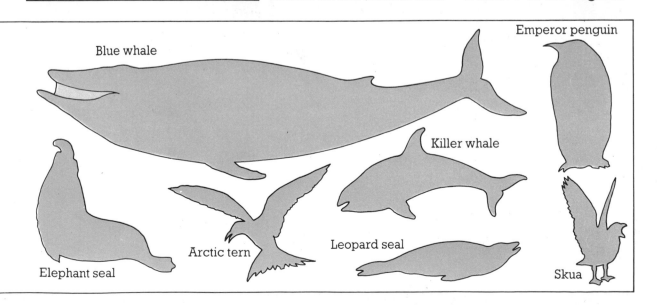

Blue whale

Emperor penguin

Killer whale

Elephant seal

Arctic tern

Leopard seal

Skua

Surviving the cold

Polar winters are severe. At the poles there is continuous darkness for six months. Thick fur protects polar bears and musk oxen from the sub-zero temperatures. Seals have thick layers of fat. Caribou migrate south, the Arctic fox stores food and the ground squirrel sleeps.

Even in summer, it is rarely above freezing at the pole. It may reach 10°C (50°F) on the tundra, but only for two or three months.

▽ An Arctic ground squirrel, or souslik, in Alaska. The Arctic souslik is a ground-living relative of the squirrels and lives throughout the tundra region. They are the only tundra mammals that hibernate (sleep through the winter). After their seven-month sleep, they emerge from their burrows in April or May to feed on shoots and insects and rear their young.

The willow ptarmigan, a kind of grouse, changes color in winter.

△ In summer, its colors match the surroundings.

◁ In winter, its plumage is white, like the snow. This helps it to hide from its enemies.

11

The great white bear

The polar bears are the largest land animals in the Arctic. These strong, fearless mammals live on the ice floes of the Arctic Ocean or on the northern shores of Alaska, Canada, Greenland, Scandinavia and the USSR. They are sometimes known as the "Lords of the Arctic."

They hunt seals, their main source of food. But they also eat fish, and they enjoy fruits and other plants of the short Arctic summer.

△ A male polar bear on an ice floe some 60 km (40 miles) off the coast of Alaska. Polar bears do not live in family groups. The male and female come together only during the mating season.

Polar bears roam far and wide. They wander over land and drift for hundreds of miles on ice floes.

They stalk their prey, mostly ringed seals, with great stealth. Almost invisible against the white background, a bear will creep slowly toward a sleeping seal until it is near enough to pounce.

▽ A polar bear enjoys the comparative warmth of a river in Canada's Northwest Territories. Polar bears are slow but strong swimmers, and may swim 30 km (20 miles) to reach an ice floe, where seals are plentiful.

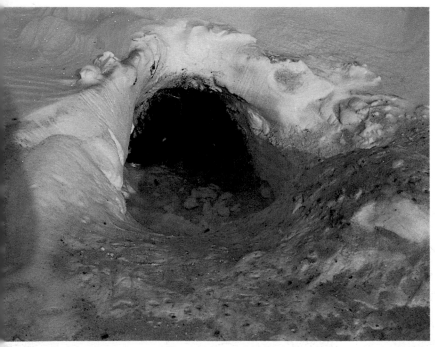

△ A mother polar bear watches her three cubs sheltering in a snow drift in the Hudson Bay area of Canada. Cubs stay with their mother until they are old enough to hunt for food themselves.

◁ The entrance of a polar bear den. As winter starts, the female bear digs a roomy den where she can have her cubs, usually two.

The hunting of polar bears has reduced their numbers. But they are now protected in most areas by law, and hunting is severely restricted. Scientists study the habits of polar bears.

▷ Polar bear cubs, which have been tranquilized, or put to sleep, are weighed.

▽ A scientist fixes a radio collar on a tranquilized bear. The bear's movements can then be followed.

Sea animals

Seals and whales are found in both polar regions. They are mammals that have adapted to life in the sea, although they come to the surface to breathe. Whales can stay underwater for as much as an hour.

Seals live on fish and other sea life. In the winter, some make breathing holes in the ice. Others make long journeys to warmer seas.

There are many kinds of seals, including sea lions and walruses.

△ A bull (male) elephant seal with mouth open is a fearsome sight. Elephant seals are the largest of the seals. A bull may weigh as much as 4 tons (8,000 lb). Southern elephant seals live in the oceans around Antarctica and breed on islands such as South Georgia.

△ A cow (female) elephant seal. The cows are about a third the size of the bulls.

▷ A young fur seal on South Georgia. Unlike the true seals, fur seals and sea lions have small, outside ears. On land, the eared seals, as they are called, use their front flippers as "legs." Their hind flippers also help them to move on land.

Seals have a thick layer of fat called blubber under their skin. This helps them keep warm in the icy cold seas and gives them energy when they cannot get food.

Several kinds of whales inhabit the polar seas. They, too, have thick layers of blubber. The blue whale is the largest animal that has ever lived.

Wales are hunted for the oil obtained from their fat.

△ A harbor, or common, seal with her pup at Glacier Bay, Alaska. Pups are born on land, but take to the water after just a few days.

△ Pacific bull walruses off the coast of south-west Alaska. Walruses live only in the Arctic region. Their long canine teeth have developed into tusks, which they use to dig up shellfish from the sea bottom. They do not eat fish.

▷ A humpback whale comes up for air in Glacier Bay, Alaska. Whales spend all of their time in the water.

Penguins

There are nearly twenty kinds of penguins, and they range from the tropics to Antarctica. They cannot fly, but are very fast underwater swimmers, and spend most of their lives in the sea. They lay their eggs and raise their young on land.

Penguins live mainly on fish and krill. Their chief enemies are leopard seals and birds called skuas, which swoop on penguin eggs and chicks.

△ Emperor penguins on an Antarctic ice shelf. These are the largest species (kind) of penguin and stand as much as 1.2 m (4 ft) high, weighing perhaps 45 kg (100 lb). During the long Antarctic winter, they hatch their eggs and raise their young on the ice.

△ King penguins gather to hatch their eggs. The female lays a single egg and her mate takes the first turn at incubation, keeping it warm by holding it between his feet and the fat of his belly.

▷ A king penguin chick begging for food. Chicks are fed by their parents for several months, and it is nearly a year before they can fend for themselves.

◁ Macaroni penguins have a dark face and chin and a yellow crest. Many types of penguins use stones in building their nests.

▽ A gentoo penguin feeding a chick. Gentoos are medium-sized penguins. They have a white flash above the eye and an orange beak.

△ Rockhopper
penguins appear to
enjoy jumping off small
rocks.

▷ An Adelie penguin
building a nest. The
male offers the female a
pebble, and if she
accepts, they build a
nest together. Adelies
sometimes walk as
much as 100 km (60
miles) across the ice to
the nesting grounds of
their colonies.

Other birds

△ An Arctic tern in flight. Terns migrate some 18,000 km (11,000 miles) between the Arctic and Antarctic.

◁ The snowy owl lives in the Arctic and hunts by day and night.

▷ A puffin, a seabird that nests in colonies on rocky Arctic coasts in the summer. It moves south for the winter.

Other polar animals

◁ Caribou, or reindeer, crossing a river on their migration across Canada's Yukon Territory. They also live in other regions of the Arctic.

▽ Musk oxen do not migrate. They have long hair over a short, woolly undercoat to protect them from the cold Arctic climate. They feed on grass, moss and other plants.

△ The Arctic fox has a grayish-brown coat in the summer which turns white in the winter. It is a scavenger, feeding on scraps left by polar bears or on dead fish and birds found on the shore.

▷ The snowshoe hare blends into the white background of the Arctic snow. It lives on plants, and sleeps on the ground in a "form," or nest. It is an important source of food for wolves and birds of prey.

The story of polar animals

Upsetting the balance

For centuries, Eskimo people have lived in harmony with their Arctic surroundings and with the animals of the region. But modern hunting methods and the search for oil and minerals threaten to upset the delicate balance of nature in both polar regions. Human interference has become a threat to the survival of many animals.

Hunting to extinction

Some species have already been hunted to extinction. One species of dugong, called Steller's sea cow, used to live in the north-western Pacific. These large sea mammals, some 10 m (33 ft) long, were hunted by islanders for hundreds of years. But the last 2,000 or so were exterminated by sailors over 200 years ago.

Seabirds have also become extinct through human greed or stupidity. The last great auk, a flightless bird that lived on the coasts of the North Atlantic, was killed in 1844.

Survival

International laws have been passed to restrict the hunting of

▽ Hunting walrus in the Arctic over 100 years ago. The walrus was killed chiefly for its ivory tusks.

△ **The great auk, now extinct.**

several polar species. Whaling for commercial purposes has been regulated. For example, the narwhal, an Arctic whale hunted for its valuable ivory tusk, is protected by a quota system: only a certain number may be killed by each hunting community.

Some of the larger whales, valued for their oil and flesh, have been hunted almost to extinction because of the difficulty in setting up and enforcing international laws on the vast oceans. Ironically, this very fact has worked against the whaling industry. The numbers of whales have been reduced so much in the last thirty years that it is no longer as profitable to mount expensive hunting expeditions. So there is hope for the whales' survival.

Polar bears, too, were seriously threatened not long ago by overhunting. But their numbers have increased as a result of strict controls.

The food chain

The animals of the polar regions are dependent on plant life and lower forms of animal life for their food. At one end of the food chain in the oceans is the phytoplankton, a tiny form of drifting plantlife nourished by the energy of the sun and the abundant mineral salts found in the cold waters. This provides food for a mass of tiny animal forms called zooplankton, which in turn provides food for fish, birds, seals and even some kinds of whales. Larger animals are then eaten by still larger ones. Penguins and seals eat fish; some seals also eat peguins. At the top of the food chain, killer whales and polar bears eat seals.

It is easy to see, then, how important the zooplankton is to the higher forms of life. So there is serious concern over plans to "harvest" the Antarctic krill, a major type of zooplankton.

Government agencies and scientists in the polar regions keep a constant watch for any such threats to the balance of nature.

Facts and records

△ An albatross in flight over its breeding ground on South Georgia.

Largest seabird

Albatrosses are regular visitors to the islands around Antarctica. These huge seabirds spend most of their lives soaring above the oceans. They come to land only to breed. The wandering albatross has the greatest wingspan of any living bird, as much as 3.6 m (11 ft 10 in).

Furry feet

The polar bear has a dense pad of fur on the sole of each foot. This helps it to walk on icy surfaces without slipping.

Longest lived mammal

Apart from human beings, the killer whale is the longest-lived mammal in the world. One specimen is known to have lived for over 90 years. The killer whale is a large porpoise, a member of the dolphin family.

Killer whales are among the fastest of all swimmers, and often travel in packs. They feed on large fish and seals, and sometimes attack walruses and even large whales.

△ The sole of a polar bear's foot is padded to keep it from slipping.

△ The killer whale is a large porpoise, or dolphin.

Glossary

Antarctica
The south polar region.

Arctic
The north polar region.

Blubber
A thick layer of fat under the skin of some animals.

Extinction
The dying out of a species (kind) of animal.

Food chain
A series of organisms that depend on one another for food; each animal in the chain is fed on by a larger one that in turn feeds a still larger one. If a species of animal or plant on the food chain is in short supply or dies out, the animals depending on it for food are also threatened.

Hibernate
To sleep through the winter, as some animals do.

Ice floe
A large piece of floating ice.

Incubation
Keeping an egg warm until it is ready to hatch.

Migration
Moving from one place to another. Large groups of mammals and birds migrate regularly to the same places at the same seasons of the year, to avoid the cold or a food shortage or both. They return later to their original homes.

Poles
The two extremes of the earth. The North Pole is located on the ice of the Arctic Ocean. The South Pole lies on the frozen continent of Antarctica.

Scavenger
An animal that feeds on scraps left by other animals or on dead animals.

Tranquilizing
A way of putting animals to sleep for a short time without harming them.

Tundra
The low plains found in the lands surrounding the Arctic Ocean. The ground is permanently frozen to a great depth except for a thin layer on top. This thaws during the summer and the tundra is richly vegetated with flowering and other plants.

Index